Amazing Animals
Polar Bears

Michael De Medeiros

W

WEIGL PUBLISHERS INC.
Forbes Media Center

Published by Weigl Publishers Inc.
350 5th Avenue, Suite 3304, PMB 6G
New York, NY 10118-0069

Amazing Animals series ©2009
WEIGL PUBLISHERS INC.
www.weigl.com

Library of Congress Cataloging-in-
Publication Data

De Medeiros, Michael.
  Polar bears / Michael De Medeiros.
    p. cm. – (Amazing animals)
  Includes index.
  ISBN 978-1-59036-964-7 (hard cover :
alk. paper) – ISBN 978-1-59036-965-4
(soft cover : alk. paper)
  1. Polar bear–Juvenile literature. I.
Title.
  QL737.C27D36 2009
  599.786–dc22

2008003762

Editor
Heather Kissock
Design and Layout
Terry Paulhus, Kathryn Livingstone

Photograph credits
Every reasonable effort has been made
to trace ownership and to obtain
permission to reprint copyright material.
The publishers would be pleased to
have any errors or omissions brought to
their attention so that they may be
corrected in subsequent printings.

All photos supplied by Getty Images.

Printed in the United States of America
1 2 3 4 5 6 7 8 9 0 12 11 10 09 08

About This Book

This book tells you all about polar bears. Find out where they live and what they eat. Discover how you can help to protect them. You can also read about them in myths and legends from around the world.

Words in **bold** are explained in the Words to Know section at the back of the book.

Useful Websites

Addresses in this book take you to the home pages of websites that have information about polar bears.

All of the Internet URLs given in the book were valid at the time of publication. However, due to the dynamic nature of the Internet, some addresses may have changed, or sites may have ceased to exist since publication. While the author and publisher regret any inconvenience this may cause readers, no responsibility for any such changes can be accepted by either the author or the publisher.

Contents

Meet the Polar Bear

Polar bears are the biggest bears in the world. Known as the "Kings of the **Arctic**," they are about the size of a small car. The polar bear is also the world's largest land **carnivore**.

Polar bears are marine **mammals**. This means that they spend much of their time in or near the ocean. Marine mammals depend on the ocean for food.

▼ Polar bears can often be seen on the ice that floats in Arctic waters.

The Bear Family

There are many different types of bears.

- black bears
- brown bears
- giant pandas
- sloth bears
- spectacled bears
- sun bears

▲ The giant panda lives on the forested mountain slopes of central China.

A Very Special Animal

Living in the Arctic requires special features.
A polar bear's coat is made up of two layers.
The inner fur is thick and woolly. It keeps the
animal warm during cold winters. The outer
coat is made of long, coarse hair. Each hair
has an oily coating that keeps off water. This
helps the polar bear dry quickly when it gets
out of the water.

▼ The skin
of a polar bear is
black. This helps
its body absorb
the Sun's heat.

Polar bears have a thick
layer of fat under their skin
that protects them from the
cold. This layer of fat is
useful in another way as
well. When there is no food,
polar bears can use the
extra fat for energy to live.

Fur that appears white in light **camouflages** the bear against the snow.

Polar bears have a very good sense of smell. It can help them find **prey** that is more than 20 miles (32 kilometers) away.

A polar bear has 42 sharp teeth that are used for protection and catching food.

Polar bears have four large paws that act like snowshoes. They help the bear stay on top of thick snow.

Curved claws are used to catch prey. They also help the bear grip the ice when walking.

Where Polar Bears Live

Polar bears can be found in the Arctic regions of Canada, the United States, Denmark, Norway, and Russia. These areas have cold weather, high winds, and icy surfaces for much of the year.

Adult male polar bears live on the snow and ice, hunting seals and other animals. Polar bear mothers live in **dens** when their cubs are young. During winter months, polar bears move south. At the beginning of summer, they travel north again, toward the North Pole.

▶ Polar bears rarely roam as far north as the North Pole because little food can be found there.

Polar Bear Range

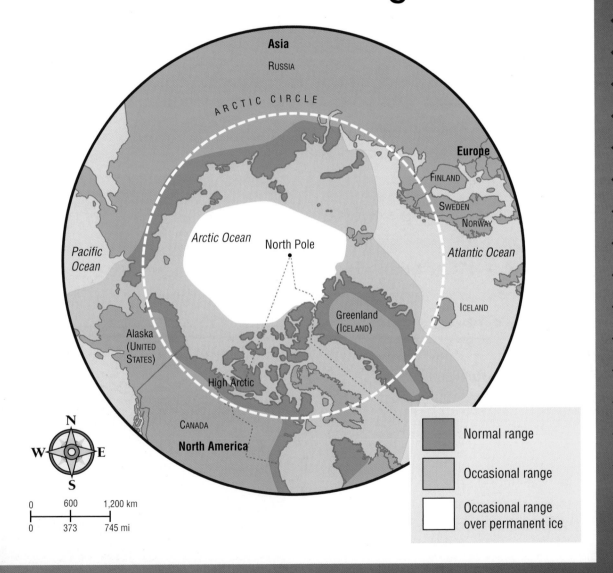

What Polar Bears Eat

A polar bear's diet is made up mainly of ringed and bearded seals. They sometimes feed on whales, walruses, ducks, fish, and other small animals as well. Plants, such as berries, are another food source for polar bears.

Polar bears have a very big stomach. Males can eat up to 100 pounds (45 kilograms) of food at one meal. Polar bears do most of their eating in the spring and early summer. They store the food in their bodies as extra fat. The fat is used to keep the bear alive when food is hard to find.

► The ringed seal is the most common seal in the Arctic.

What a Meal!

- Polar bears have different ways of hunting. The most common is called still hunting. The bear stays very still by a seal's breathing hole. When the seal comes up for air, the bear bites it and pulls it from the water.

- A polar bear does not always eat the meat of its kill. It prefers the skin and fat layers.

▲ Polar bears sometimes go hunting in the water.

Growing Up

At birth, a polar bear cub weighs about 1 pound (0.5 kg) and is no bigger than a small house cat. Newborn cubs cannot see or hear and have no teeth.

▼ Cubs learn to walk when they are about eight weeks old.

In the first month, cubs grow to be four times larger than the size they were at birth. They can now see and hear. The cubs stay in their den for about three months and depend on their mother for food and protection. When they are about four months old, the cubs leave the den with their mother to learn how to hunt. The cubs will stay with their mother for at least two years.

Growth Chart

Birth	1 pound (0.5 kg)	Cubs have little fur, no teeth, and cannot see or hear.
1 month old	4 pounds (2 kg)	Cubs can see and hear.
2 months old	22 to 26 pounds (10 to 12 kg)	Cubs grow teeth and thick white fur.
8 to 12 months old	99 pounds (45 kg)	Cubs begin eating solid food and learning to hunt.
24 to 36 months old	221 to 675 pounds (100 to 306 kg)	Cubs leave their mother's care.
10 to 11 years old	500 to 1,000 pounds (227 to 454 kg)	The bears are full-grown adults.

▼ Polar bears give birth to two or three cubs at a time.

Polar Bear Dens

Before a polar bear cub is born, its mother builds a den. The mother rests in the den while waiting for her cubs to arrive. The den protects the mother and her cubs from the cold and other animals. Dens are usually 4 feet (1.2 meters) across and 3 feet (0.9 m) high. Some dens have three or four rooms.

Male polar bears do not stay with mothers and cubs. They wander throughout their home area and continue to hunt.

▶ Dens can be on land or on sea ice. They are usually built into a snowdrift.

Inside Mom's Den

- To keep the cold wind away, the mother polar bear digs a long tunnel in the snow. This tunnel leads to the den.

- In the months leading up to birth, mother polar bears do not eat or drink. They lose almost half their weight during this time.

Friends and Enemies

Polar bears spend most of their time alone. They sometimes form small groups during mating season or when a mother is raising her cubs. When together, polar bears can be very playful. They chase one another and wrestle for fun.

▼ When polar bears fight, it is usually for a mate.

Humans are the polar bear's main threat. They hunt the bears for food and to use their fur for clothing. Air and water pollution caused by humans is also affecting the polar bear's **habitat**.

Useful Websites

http://animals.national geographic.com

Click on "Animals of the Arctic" to find information on other animals that live near polar bears.

Living with Polar Bears

There are many different animals that live in the same places as polar bears.

- eider ducks
- lemmings
- Arctic foxes
- seals
- walruses
- whales

▲ Arctic fox often follow a polar bear and eat the remains of the bear's meals.

Under Threat

The are fewer polar bears living in the Arctic than there used to be. This is mainly because of **global warming**. The bear's natural habitat is melting, leaving the bear with reduced hunting grounds and fewer animals to hunt.

The polar bear is considered one of the world's most **threatened** animals. In the next 50 years, the number of polar bears in the world is expected to decline by about one third.

▼ Oil drilling in the Arctic is affecting polar bear habitat. Pipelines are being built where polar bears build their dens.

Useful Websites

www.polarbears international.org

Visit this website to learn about how people are trying to help save polar bears.

What Do You Think?

Some polar bears live in zoos. The zoos help increase the polar bear population, but they also keep bears in spaces much smaller than their normal habitat. Should polar bears be held in captivity? Should they be free in their natural habitat?

▲ Tourists can disrupt the polar bear's habitat and cause changes in the way polar bears behave.

Myths and Legends

For thousands of years, the Aboriginal Peoples of the Arctic have lived alongside the polar bear. They have viewed the bear with both respect and fear. They called the polar bear *Nanook*, which means "ever-wandering one."

These people noticed that they had much in common with the polar bear. Like humans, the bear is able to stand on its back legs. It builds dens that look like **igloos**. Polar bears even eat the same food as Arctic peoples. For this reason, Aboriginal Peoples have many legends in which the polar bear is able to become human.

▶ Some igloos hold only two or three people. Others can house up to 20 people.

The Inuit of Canada's North believed that the polar bear had strong magical powers. Inuit medicine men often tried to get the polar bear to be their protector. They performed a special ceremony in order to do this. If the polar bear agreed to be a medicine man's protector, the man could use the polar bear's magic to help his people.

▶ The medicine man would walk deep into the Arctic wilderness and call the polar bear to him so that he could ask it to be his protector.

Quiz

1. Where do polar bears live?
   (a) **the Antarctic** (b) **the Arctic** (c) **the tropics**

2. How long does a cub stay in the den?
   (a) **three months** (b) **six months** (c) **two years**

3. How many teeth does a polar bear have?
   (a) **24** (b) **42** (c) **50**

4. What animal makes up most of a polar bear's diet?
   (a) **Arctic fox** (b) **seal** (c) **walrus**

5. How many countries do polar bears live in?
   (a) **two** (b) **three** (c) **five**

Answers:
1. (b) Polar bears live in the Arctic.
2. (a) Polar bears stay in the den for the first three months of their life.
3. (b) A polar bear has 42 teeth.
4. (b) Polar bears eat mostly seals.
5. (c) Polar bears are found in five countries.

22

Find out More

To find out more about polar bears, visit the websites in this book. You can also write to these organizations.

Arctic Studies Center
P.O. Box 37012
Department of Anthropology (MRC112)
National Museum of Natural History
Smithsonian Institution
Washington, DC 20013-7012

Polar Bear SOS
Natural Resources Defense Council
40 West 20th Street
New York, NY 10011

World Wildlife Fund
United States
1250 24th Street N.W.
Washington, DC 20037

Words to Know

Arctic
the region around the North Pole

camouflages
helps an animal blend in with
its environment

carnivore
an animal that mainly eats meat

dens
places where polar bears give birth
and raise their young

global warming
an increase in Earth's temperature

habitat
the natural area where animals live

igloos
domed houses made out of snow

mammals
animals that have hair or fur and feed
milk to their young

prey
animals that are hunted by other animals
for food

threatened
an animal that is at risk of disappearing
from Earth

Index